Photographing
GRAND CANYON

Where, When, and How to Capture the Best Photos

BY **Gary Ladd**

GRAND CANYON CONSERVANCY

Founded in 1932, the Grand Canyon Conservancy is the National Park Service's official nonprofit partner, raising private funds to benefit Grand Canyon National Park, operating park stores and visitor centers within the park, and providing premier educational opportunities about the natural and cultural history of the region. The Grand Canyon Conservancy works to inspire people to protect and enhance Grand Canyon National Park for present and future generations. Proceeds from the sale of this book directly support the mission of Grand Canyon National Park.

For more information on the Grand Canyon Conservancy or to become a member, visit www.grandcanyon.org.

Grand Canyon Conservancy
P.O. Box 399, Grand Canyon, AZ 86023
(800) 858-2808
www.grandcanyon.org

Copyright © 2016 Grand Canyon Conservancy
Text and photographs copyright © 2016 Gary Ladd

ISBN 978-1-934656-77-8

No portion of this book may be reproduced in whole or in part, by any means (with the exception of short quotes for the purpose of review), without permission of the publisher.

Printed in Korea

Designed by David Jenney Design
Edited by Faith Marcovecchio

Rocks are not merely beautiful; they are loaded with ancient messages. This book is dedicated to Earth's geologic history, the men and women who cunningly unlock that history, and the elegant (and highly photogenic!) evidence tucked away in Earth's rocks, mountains, mesas, and canyon cliffs…especially Grand Canyon.

CONTENTS

Introduction **1**
Map: South Rim **2**
Map: North Rim **4**

6

SUNSET

SOUTH RIM
  Mather Point **7**
  Hopi Point **7**
  Mojave Point **8**
  Yaki Point **8**
  Lipan Point **8**
  Navajo Point **11**
  Desert View **11**

NORTH RIM
  Bright Angel Point **12**
  Cape Royal **12**

14

SUNRISE

SOUTH RIM
  Mather Point
    to Yavapai Point **15**
  Hopi Point
    and Powell Point **15**
  Pima Point **15**
  Duck on a Rock **16**
  Moran Point **17**

NORTH RIM
  Point Imperial **18**
  Cape Royal **19**

20

MIDDAY

Canyon **21**
Plants and Animals **23**

26 WEATHER

- Clouds 27
- Rainbows 30
- Snow 31
- Wild Cards 32

34 PEOPLE

- On the Rim 35
- Portraits 37

38 TECHNIQUE

- Foregrounds 39
- Rule of Thirds 44
- Framing 45
- Focal Length 46
- Patterns and Graphic Lines 48
- Shadows and Silhouettes 50
- Backlighting 52
- Sun Stars 53
- God Rays 54

Creating a Slide Show 56
Grand Canyon Facts 57
Epilogue 58

INTRODUCTION

GRAND CANYON is one of Earth's most glorious and dramatic landscapes. It's no surprise that many of us want to take a little bit of that drama home with us. Making photos of the canyon is an excellent way to do exactly that.

But the canyon challenges us to capture it favorably. That's because there are *two* Grand Canyons. The first one is the physical spectacle in front of you. The second is created by your camera, a related but altered rendering of Grand Canyon.

It's your job to translate the first into the second in a pleasing way. To do this, you must employ the positive aspects of photography to overcome the negatives of the art form and the canyon's peculiarities to make images that, although not completely faithful, are inspiring and would charm a person looking at the real Grand Canyon. Using techniques such as careful composition, photography's greater contrast when compared with the human eye, combinations of foreground and background, and good timing, you can make images that can compete with reality—simply because they focus the viewer's perception on something interesting.

In many ways, you already know how to make pleasing photos of Grand Canyon because you've practiced photographic techniques elsewhere. You know to look for strong compositions and take advantage of good light. You may already be a disciple of "the rule of thirds" or use close-ups and abstractions to make your photos more powerful. I'll show you how to take those techniques and put them to good use at the canyon.

Your camera will help you. Until recently, almost no one who visited Grand Canyon possessed the incredible array of photographic tools you have in your hands: camera phone convenience, fast and effective computer-aided image enhancement, instant photo transmission, as well as more sophisticated tools such as image stabilization, astonishingly sharp zoom lenses, digital image capture at high ISO settings, and more. With all this new firepower, a few suggestions and ideas are all you need to take great Grand Canyon images.

This guide offers the where, when, and how. It names the best places to go, the ultimate times to take photos, and the most interesting ways to capture Grand Canyon's many moods. It bumps up your repertoire of image variety. In short, this book will help you get the most photographically out of your Grand Canyon visit.

What this book won't do is get bogged down in the technical aspects of digital photography. Lots other books have covered those topics in detail; I focus on Grand Canyon rim photography.

It's a subject I know well. I've been taking pictures of Grand Canyon for more than fifty years and have literally spent several years on the canyon's rims, hiking and backpacking its trails, and floating the Colorado River in its depths. I've had some of the best times of my life doing it.

I hope that you, too, will have time to explore the canyon's rims, savor the canyon's beauty, and produce your own unique images of this spectacular place.

GARY LADD

SOUTH RIM MAP

PIMA POINT

HOPI POINT

MATHER POINT

YAKI POINT

MOJAVE POINT

DUCK ON A ROCK

NORTH RIM

Hermits Rest
Pima Point
Monument Creek Vista
The Abyss
Mojave Point
Trailview Overlook
Hopi Point
Powell Point
Maricopa Point
Bright Angel Trailhead
Yavapai Point
Mather Point
South Kaibab Trailhead
Yaki Point
Grand Canyon Village
Grand Canyon Visitor Center
Village Drive
Center Road
Desert View Drive
South Entrance Station
Duck on a Rock

SOUTH RIM

64

Cape Royal

SUNSET

It's a Grand Canyon tradition to experience sunset on the rim. Usually, I look for mostly clear skies on the horizon in the direction of the sun so that beams of light can fly across the canyon. But I also hope to see broken clouds above and away from the direction of the sun so that the sky itself, not just the canyon, is covered in interesting and colorful structural elements.

   Arrive early. It's easier to anticipate the look of the sky and the canyon in the hour before sunset, giving you time to scout out the location and identify the best view directions and foreground elements. It's wise to hang around for at least half an hour after sunset, too, to see what develops. Because many cameras are shockingly effective at low light levels, the time after sunset can sometimes produce the strongest images. Try not to let dinner get in the way; carry some snacks to tide you over. If you have one, use a tripod.

Mather Point

SUNSET | SOUTH RIM

Hopi Point

MATHER POINT—Even though Mather Point is the largest, most developed overlook in all of Grand Canyon, in many ways, it's also the best.

✿ Spectacular eastern views of monumental temples are silhouetted against the horizon.

✿ O'Neill Butte, northeast of the overlook, catches red light before sunset, ideal for a strong foreground element.

✿ Although Mather Point is often crowded, the visitors themselves can be appealing elements in your photos.

✿ There's lots of parking, excellent shuttle service from all directions, a beautifully remodeled viewing area, and the Visitor Center and Park Store are nearby.

HOPI POINT—Hopi Point juts far out into the canyon with completely unobstructed views east and west, and therefore it's become a well-known spot for viewing sunset. To get there, you'll need to use the free Hermits Rest Route shuttle bus heading west on Hermit Road.

✿ To the east there are excellent views of two distant but imposing Grand Canyon temples that stand in silhouette against the horizon.

✿ To the west, segments of the Colorado River are visible in Upper Granite Gorge.

> Mather Point parking can become extremely congested on summer afternoons. Arrive early for sunset to secure a parking place or use the free shuttles.

SUNSET | SOUTH RIM

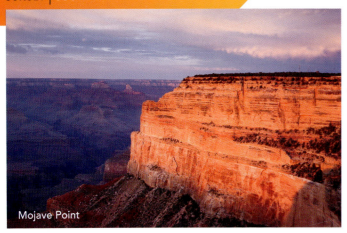

Mojave Point

Yaki Point

MOJAVE POINT—Several discrete vantage points, with and without railings, are available at Mojave Point. Use the free Hermits Rest Route shuttle bus for access to Mojave Point.

▣ Features an unparalleled view of the massive cliff below Hopi Point, a formation that glows incandescent orange at sunset in the summer months.

▣ Unobstructed views of the canyon's complex interior, especially to the north and northwest, including a great perspective of Hermit Rapid, one of the biggest river-runner "roller-coaster rides" in all of Grand Canyon.

YAKI POINT—Yaki Point features wide-open panoramas east and west. Use the Kaibab/Rim Route shuttle bus to get there.

▣ Here's the best view of the South Kaibab Trail as it zigzags down into the canyon depths below and beyond O'Neill Butte to the north.

▣ It's an easy walk eastward along the rim from the overlook, a good chance to get away from the crowds.

▣ You can use the same shuttle bus to get to the South Kaibab trailhead.

LIPAN POINT—This overlook is my most productive overlook on the South Rim's east end.

▣ Fine views northeastward up the Colorado River as it emerges from Marble Canyon.

▣ More vistas eastward toward the imposing sunset-illuminated cliffs of the Palisades of the Desert.

▣ Best of all are the staggering western views toward the setting summer sun, particularly photogenic when there are high clouds to the west.

SUNSET | SOUTH RIM

Lipan Point

When photographing toward the setting sun, it can be difficult to overcome contrast between light and dark areas. The inner canyon becomes murky, almost invisible. Clouds help alleviate the problem by bouncing light into the shadows, and photos with clouds can be very dramatic. But sometimes it's best and easiest to seek scenes that lie roughly 90 degrees away from the sun, where the sky is not so overwhelmingly bright and the inner canyon presents a mixture of sunlit and shadowed cliffs.

SUNSET | SOUTH RIM

Navajo Point

SUNSET | SOUTH RIM

Desert View

NAVAJO POINT—Navajo Point lies between Lipan Point and Desert View. Like its neighbors, Navajo Point features dynamite views to the west, north, and northeast. There's usually lots of parking because the facilities at Desert View draw the majority of visitors.

- Magnificent views down the canyon's length to the west, where segments of the Colorado River glint in the afternoon sun.

- Views up the Colorado River to the north are also impressive late in the day.

DESERT VIEW—Desert View is the main overlook at the eastern end of the canyon, South Rim, with the convenience of a large parking area, visitor center, campground, and gas station.

- Staggering views to the west, north, and northwest, especially as sunset approaches.

- Handsome Desert View Watchtower can be incorporated into some of your Grand Canyon scenes.

SUNSET | NORTH RIM

Bright Angel Point

BRIGHT ANGEL POINT— The North Rim has far fewer overlooks than the South Rim, and they tend to be more widely separated. However, several are particularly remarkable.

The quarter-mile walk from the Grand Canyon Lodge to the tip of Bright Angel Point offers lovely views in several directions, especially to the southwest, south, southeast, and northeast.

- Great views across the canyon toward Oza Butte, Brahma Temple, and Zoroaster Temple.

- Railed overlooks immediately below and near the lodge can be used as appealing foreground elements when photographed from the walkways above them.

CAPE ROYAL— Cape Royal is one of Grand Canyon's treasures, wonderful for both sunrise and sunset with its 270-degree view of the canyon. A half-mile trail leads through the forest to views of Angels Window, a stately natural arch carved from the rim rock. Give yourself plenty of time to get to Cape Royal; it's a 45-minute drive from Grand Canyon Lodge, plus the trail walk.

- Wonderful views with majestic temples rising from the canyon floor.

- A picnic area at the southwest tip of the parking lot offers fantastic views of the canyon to the southwest if you wish to get away from the crowds.

- Angels Window can be used to frame the canyon and, if you find the right spot, a segment of the Colorado River.

Cape Royal

SUNRISE

A compelling sunrise shot of the canyon is a worthy goal: The combination of canyon and rising sun is one of primal power.

If possible, scout out your location beforehand to identify the best views and foreground elements. The next morning, arrive early. Every sunrise is different, and you may need to make location adjustments for this particular day's arrival.

I prefer locations that offer me a great sunward view to the east. Though more difficult to capture, into-the-sun images are dramatic. I sometimes use graduated neutral density filters or image-processing software to help with the contrast.

A tripod allows longer exposures in the dim pre-sunrise light and smaller apertures to incorporate foreground elements without fear of fuzzy focus.

While looking toward the sun, keep an eye on what's happening in other directions as the light sweeps deeper into the canyon.

At dawn, conditions are changing fast. If you can, work until an hour after sunrise, when the rate of change dwindles. Don't go rushing off to breakfast—pull out those snacks and watch what happens!

Mather Point

SUNRISE | SOUTH RIM

Hopi Point

Pima Point

MATHER TO YAVAPAI POINT—Almost any location between Yavapai Point and Mather Point is great at sunrise. This rim segment is unusually photogenic, because the paved Greenway Trail follows the rim here, allowing photographers to capture uncluttered, unobstructed views from the trail.

- Superb views eastward toward Wotans Throne and Vishnu Temple.

- In midsummer, the sun comes up from behind Wotans Throne, adding extra drama to the scene.

HOPI AND POWELL POINT—Hopi Point and Powell Point are close together, so the distant views are comparable. They are both accessible by the Hermits Rest Route shuttle bus.

- Hopi Point is my favorite of the two, only because I can sometimes employ a telephoto lens to capture visitors standing at Powell Point as foreground elements.

- Both overlooks offer dramatic silhouettes of Wotans Throne and Vishnu Temple to the east, toward the rising sun, especially in the summer months.

PIMA POINT—Pima Point offers the last excellent views on Hermit Road. (Farther west, at Hermits Rest, the canyon views to the east are largely hidden.)

- Pima Point views are especially appealing to the northwest, where the Colorado River is visible in the sweeping Upper Granite Gorge.

- To the northeast there's a clear view of Granite Rapid. (During one early morning visit to Pima Point I could clearly hear the roar of the rapid and the screams of river runners plunging through it.)

SUNRISE | SOUTH RIM

Duck on a Rock

DUCK ON A ROCK—Duck on a Rock is an old overlook with a paved pull-off. It is approximately three miles east of the Yaki Point turnoff on Desert View Drive. Duck on the Rock possesses three valuable features:

- It's not a famous overlook, so it's almost never crowded.

- A rock hoodoo, or tower, stands in front of the overlook, offering an interesting foreground ingredient.

- The barbed summit of Vishnu Temple dominates the distant horizon.

> Sunrises on clear days are always difficult when looking into the sun, but sunrises on days when there are clouds over the canyon create drama in the sky, a brightening of the interior of the canyon, and, sometimes, rays fanning out from the sun. Attempt these photos only if you know how to handle the extreme contrast. (To accurately gauge your results, you must consult your LCD screen and histogram.) If you haven't photographed into the sun before, it's better to concentrate on scenes that do not include the sun.

MORAN POINT—I would suggest that instead of visiting Grandview Point (which, despite its name, rates only as an average photography site), visit Moran Point.

◘ By walking east from the parking area, you can get away from most of the crowds at the main overlook without losing fruitful views.

◘ The flat-topped castle of rock just beyond the overlook makes a nice foreground element.

◘ It's less difficult to find a parking place at Moran than Lipan and (especially) Grandview.

Moran Point

SUNRISE | NORTH RIM

Point Imperial

POINT IMPERIAL—Point Imperial is often glorious at sunrise. It's located reasonably close to the Grand Canyon Lodge and the campground, with lots of parking. Allow about 30 minutes to drive there.

- At 8,803 feet, Point Imperial is the highest location on the rim of Grand Canyon, with unobstructed views to the east. It can also be quite windy, so be prepared.

- The view to the southeast is dominated by Mount Hayden, a made-for-photography pinnacle looming above a maze of chasms.

SUNRISE | NORTH RIM

Cape Royal

CAPE ROYAL— Cape Royal is terrific at sunrise for the same reason it is at sunset: 270-degree views of the canyon. Plan ahead: It's at least a 45-minute drive from Grand Canyon Lodge.

- This is a fine place to watch the day develop within the depths of the canyon.
- Because of the long drive, at sunrise you'll have Grand Canyon almost to yourself.
- Typically, the strongest photos are created at the tip of the point. You'll see Angels Window, in silhouette at sunrise, along the way.

> Sunrise: I try to arrive early enough that I can witness the day assembling, hoping for a great mix of clouds and color, watching the fast-changing light, trying to catch the scene at its most photogenic.

MIDDAY

Quite honestly, the canyon can look pretty boring when it's midday and the sky is cloudless, especially in the summer months. Midday photos tend to look colorless and bland. You don't want this as a photograph! An extremely effective solution to the "same-boring-stuff syndrome" is to incorporate foreground objects in many of your midday images. The vastness of the Grand Canyon can still dominate your scene, but the foreground features—gnarled tree trunks, cacti, jutting rim rocks—will add important counterpoints of color and form. (For more on foregrounds, see pages 39–43.)

   Midday also allows you an opportunity to capture some photogenic features on the rim that should become a part of your Grand Canyon photo collection. These include plants, animals, striking patterns on rock surfaces, interesting or historic National Park Service signs, and other close-ups. You can also slow down on the photography when the light is poor. Take a break, have some lunch, explore the Visitor Center, attend a park ranger talk, or hike a ways down one of the trails.

MIDDAY | CANYON

NO FOREGROUND

WITH FOREGROUND ELEMENT

NO FOREGROUND

WITH FOREGROUND ELEMENT

Canyon

It may useful to think of your approach to Grand Canyon photography as *using the canyon as a fabulous backdrop*. By including a foreground element, such as a nearby ridge, trees and bushes, or people standing on the rim, you will add more color and interest, as well as lend depth to the scene. Foreground objects are often within a few feet of each other, so it's easy to modify your photo by moving left or right a yard or two. Effectively, you have tremendous freedom to choose those features that lie nearby, unlike the distant canyon features. Use this power!

MIDDAY | PLANTS & ANIMALS

Plants

Plants are excellent photographic subjects because they depart from the canyon's vast expanses of ancient, solid rock. Look for blooming bushes or cacti with bold shapes, twisted juniper trees, golden aspen leaves in autumn, blooming high-desert flowers, and interesting succulents—especially as you explore rim trails away from developed areas. Here are some of my favorite plants and places:

- Yellow buckwheat plants along the edge of the canyon at North Rim's Cape Royal in late summer.

- Agave plants with their geometric, needle-tipped leaves, scattered in locations along the South Rim.

- The brilliant yellow, showy rabbitbrush displays, especially at Desert View in late summer and early fall.

- Prickly pear cacti blooms in the spring, in various places, often in colonies, usually where it's open and sunny.

MIDDAY | PLANTS & ANIMALS

MIDDAY | PLANTS & ANIMALS

Animals

At midday, you may not see Grand Canyon's larger animals—elk or deer—but keep an eye out for chipmunks and ground squirrels, condors and ravens. Their antics are highly photogenic; just be sure not to feed them!

- Chipmunks and ground squirrels are most visible where there are lots of visitors careless with food scraps, commonly along the rim near Bright Angel Lodge, El Tovar Hotel, Yavapai Geology Museum, and Desert View. Use your telephoto lens but absolutely don't feed the animals or tease them with the possibility of food. They can and do inflict serious bites!

- Deer and elk are common along the South Rim. As usual, use your telephoto lens; do not approach these wild animals. Elk are especially dangerous. Do not block the park roads with your car while observing wildlife or making images.

WEATHER

Of all of my finest photographs, the ones that hold the most appeal were taken under extraordinary weather conditions: lightning storms, fog banks, angry clouds with arresting shapes. Unusual or rare natural phenomena will elevate your photos into extraordinary territory. So, when the weather deteriorates, grab your camera!

Clouds are a huge part of weather's photographic appeal. Arizona experiences a summer monsoon season from mid-July to mid-September when a few scattered morning clouds often evolve into black rain clouds and rainbows in the afternoon. The drama of storms will definitely enhance your Grand Canyon photos. (I really feel sorry for the poor visitors who see the canyon only in the middle of the day and only when the sky is cloudless—they're being robbed!)

Mother Nature sprinkles us with haphazard conditions and situations as we stand on the canyon's rim. It's your job as a discerning photographer to sort through the day's conditions and select the best combination of factors that will contribute to a pleasing image.

Clouds

There are really two Grand Canyons—one of them exists under cloudy skies, the other under clear skies. Skies with some clouds are far better for photography because clouds:

- Add structural patterns to the sky.
- Send appealing shadows into the canyon that add depth and dimension to the inner canyon.
- Reduce inner-canyon contrast between sunlit cliffs and shadowed cliffs.
- Block direct sunlight from falling on dust particles floating through the air between the canyon's temples and your camera, thereby reducing the normally undesirable effect of haze.
- Early and late in the day they can add color—pink, red, gray, silver—to canyon scenes.

Even the middle of the day can look far better photographically if clouds are about. If clouds are present, take full advantage of them.

> Polarizing filters are not always needed for landscape photography. Although they are sometimes fabulously effective for darkening skies when capturing landscape scenes located around 90 degrees from the sun, and for reducing reflections from water and other surfaces, polarizers also degrade images by sucking up light (usually two to three f-stops' worth), compelling the use of longer shutter speeds or wider apertures. Don't keep your polarizing filter on at all times. Use it only when it helps!

WEATHER | CLOUDS

WEATHER | CLOUDS

WEATHER | RAINBOWS

When you hear thunder close by, take cover; lightning storms on the canyon rim are serious business. Seek shelter inside your car, a building, or a shuttle bus—do not stand under a tree.

Rainbows

The best photo opportunities are almost always fleeting! Like rainbows: If storm clouds bring them, use a polarizing filter to enrich their colors.

◘ For a rainbow to materialize, rain must be falling in the direction opposite the sun, the sun must be shining on the rain, and you must be paying attention.

◘ Most South Rim overlooks are great locations for capturing rainbows over the canyon because many of the canyon views are directly away from the sun, just where rainbows could form.

◘ Mather Point is especially fine for rainbow-spotting because afternoon storms pass over the rim headed northeast (getting you soaked) then charge out over the canyon opposite the sun's location.

◘ At Grand Canyon, rainbows can appear *below* you, deep within the canyon.

◘ Be extremely careful when lightning is present—you *must* protect yourself by getting indoors or into your car.

Snow

Photographic opportunities unimagined by summer visitors transform the rim environment in winter. Look for the following:

- Foreground trees wrapped in shrouds of snow in counterpoint to the "summery" inner canyon a mile below.

- Buildings draped with snow; roads and walkways blanketed.

- Fog and mist drifting through the canyon.

But, there are challenges:

- The contrast between brilliant snow (especially when it's sunlit) and inner canyon can be devilishly difficult to handle—it's sometimes best when the rim snows are partially or fully shaded by trees or are under cloud cover.

- The best photo opportunities usually begin to appear as winter storms clear and in the hours immediately after.

- Transportation along the rim, by vehicle or on foot, is slower and more difficult, at least for a while—and it can be icy. To be safe, wear over-the-shoe traction devices.

- Cold makes camera batteries sluggish and freezes fingers.

Wild Cards

When conditions are "bad," look for wild cards. You'll discover these fleeting opportunities if you are observant—and lucky:

- Colorful umbrellas.
- Hair blowing in the gusty wind.
- Fog on the rim.
- Draperies of rain hanging over the canyon.
- Puddles of water in the foreground that reflect the sky, people, and trees.

Observe carefully; these moments can disappear quickly, in just a second or two, like a curtain opening suddenly then closing abruptly. I've been most surprised by the occasional instance when the best picture potential dwells not in what I hope for but in its opposite. Such situations are cruel, even diabolical. Some examples:

- I sincerely wish that the cluster of visitors on the rim in front of me would get out of my way…then realize their clothing colors are irresistible.
- I devoutly plead that clouds will cover the sun so that I can get my shot… then awaken to an even better image, backlit, possible only by looking toward the sun.
- I cry out into the high winds, begging for mercy, hoping they will subside so that I may capture a close-up of a beautiful flower…then realize the winds are covering the ground with magnificent leaves.

The takeaway: Stay on your toes, even when the situation appears grim. Sometimes the best is embedded in the worst.

WEATHER | WILD CARDS

33

PEOPLE

On the Rim

Grand Canyon images that include people standing on the rim are effective because they offer scale, intriguing shapes and silhouettes, a different palette of colors, and little pleasantries such as people-to-people and people-to-canyon interactions that the canyon alone cannot provide.

◘ For this type of image, move 25, 50, 100, or even 200 feet way away from the rim and use your telephoto lens. The long lens will magnify the canyon's details while allowing you to work unobtrusively with the figures in the foreground.

◘ Keep an eye on people who have scrambled out on ledges and the tips of prominent points. Photograph them in their precarious positions with the canyon as a backdrop. They will appear tiny and exceedingly vulnerable against the indifferent immensity of the canyon.

◘ Be patient and be fast! People are always shuffling around, assuming new poses and groupings, most of them unappealing, some of them just unexpectedly great. (It's kind of fun to do this.)

PEOPLE | ON THE RIM

PEOPLE | PORTRAITS

Get above your subjects by standing on a rock, a bench, or an upper overlook to be able to look down into the canyon behind your subjects.

Look for opportunities to position some of your subjects seated to avoid "The Lineup Look."

Try positioning your subjects diagonally for a more pleasing composition.

If your camera offers a fill-flash setting, use it in the shade with the sunlit canyon beyond. A backlight camera setting sometimes works, too.

Portraits

You can't photograph Grand Canyon without including family and friends in some close-up people shots.

These family portraits were taken at Mather Point, the most easily accessible viewpoint in the park.

◘ Avoid using wide-angle lenses. Choose normal and mild telephoto lenses to avoid facial distortion. This will also allow you to back off from your models. (Most of us don't like having cameras shoved in our faces.)

◘ Position your people so that they aren't looking directly into the sun. If they are, they're going to look squinty and unhappy. Suggest that they remove their sunglasses.

◘ With the sun now to your side, everyone should look more natural. If the best angle puts the sun behind your subjects, switch on your camera's backlight feature. Or, if your camera offers a fill-flash mode, switch it on now.

◘ Important: Be absolutely sure that your camera's autofocus sensor is targeting people, not the distant canyon walls.

◘ If you feel the need to use a wide-angle lens to include more of the canyon, position your models away from the edges of the frame to minimize misshapen heads and ill-proportioned bodies.

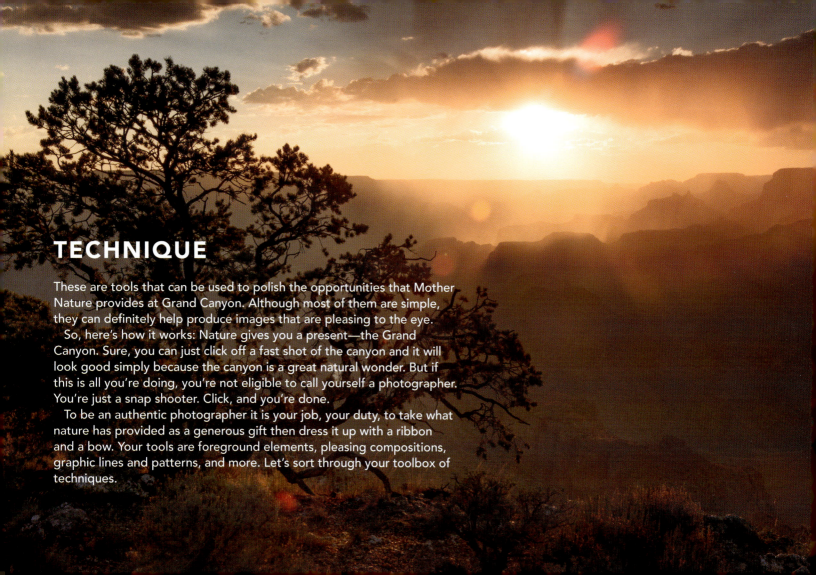

TECHNIQUE

These are tools that can be used to polish the opportunities that Mother Nature provides at Grand Canyon. Although most of them are simple, they can definitely help produce images that are pleasing to the eye.

So, here's how it works: Nature gives you a present—the Grand Canyon. Sure, you can just click off a fast shot of the canyon and it will look good simply because the canyon is a great natural wonder. But if this is all you're doing, you're not eligible to call yourself a photographer. You're just a snap shooter. Click, and you're done.

To be an authentic photographer it is your job, your duty, to take what nature has provided as a generous gift then dress it up with a ribbon and a bow. Your tools are foreground elements, pleasing compositions, graphic lines and patterns, and more. Let's sort through your toolbox of techniques.

Foregrounds

Incorporating foreground elements into your photos will add depth to your scenes, giving viewers the sense of actually being there. Foregrounds lend a wider range of contrast, shape, color, and sharp details not muted and blurred by canyon distances. Not all locations possess useful foregrounds, but if one is available, you won't want to overlook it.

Here are several important foreground concepts:

○ **JUTTING RIM ROCKS**—Rim rocks are still part of the canyon, but they provide your scene with illumination, lines, scale, contours, and details in contrast to those of the inner canyon. I often choose a vertical format so that I can include more of the jutting rim rock in the foreground. This allows the camera to look downward and outward in the same scene, thus embracing a wider variety of illumination, color, and shape to give the photo its look of space and distance.

○ **TREE TRUNKS AND ARCHING BRANCHES**—Trees, tree trunks, and tree branches can frame the scene, lending depth and, if the day is cloudless, some form in the top of your frame where otherwise there would be only a poisonously dull sky.

○ **A NEARBY RIDGE OF ROCK AND TREES**—The ridge (a rocky extension of the rim) should to be about 100 to 500 feet from your camera position with a view of the canyon beyond. From your chosen location, rocks and trees on the ridge can be shown in silhouette against the canyon's backdrop.

○ **BUSHES OR CACTI**—Away from the more developed parts of the rims, you'll find bushes with interesting shapes, cacti—which are spectacular when in bloom—and other plants to give your photos a strong foreground element.

Whenever I identify a canyon scene that appeals to me, I immediately look for a foreground element that I can use in conjunction with it. Useful foregrounds are not always present. See what's available.

TECHNIQUE | FOREGROUNDS

TECHNIQUE | FOREGROUNDS

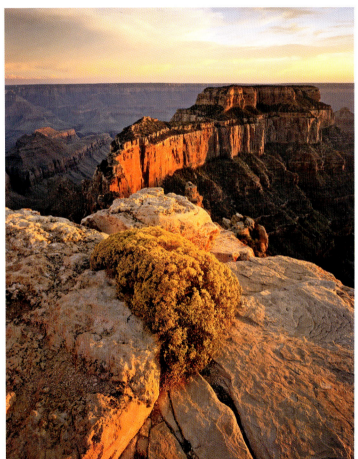

TECHNIQUE | FOREGROUNDS

Foreground Rocks

A pattern of bedrock cracks adds interest to an otherwise standard rendering of the canyon. Some extraneous sky has also been eliminated by including a foreground.

Natural Frame

Adding a natural frame of trees on the rim counterpoints the hot, treeless depths of the Grand Canyon.

TECHNIQUE | FOREGROUNDS

TECHNIQUE | RULE OF THIRDS

Rule of Thirds

The rule of thirds guides photographers on the desirability of offsetting important features from a central position in the frame. (Most of the time.)

- If your scene has a single important feature, do *not* shoot at it as if aiming for a bull's-eye. Photography shooting and target shooting are different!

- As you compose your photo, mentally divide the scene into three parts horizontally and three parts vertically. Don't center the subject; think about where the lines intersect, and place your subject near that intersection.

- I don't use the rule of thirds as an unchallengeable law; it's more a reminder that I have compositional options, one of which will almost certainly be best.

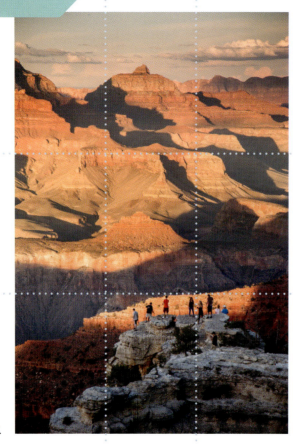

TECHNIQUE | FRAMING

Framing

A frame of tree limbs, the window frame or porch of a building, even the bodies of people can add interest and depth to a scene.

- It may help to get down low, maybe on your knees, to find a frame. (Have you ever made a shot through your dog's legs? Or beneath and between flowers?) Cameras with articulating LCD screens are terrifically effective for these kinds of shots.

- Openings in rock formations such as Angels Window on the North Rim can provide a unique view of Grand Canyon.

- Use a wide-angle lens when extra depth of focus is needed.

TECHNIQUE | FOCAL LENGTH

Telephoto

Telephoto

Focal Length

Lenses of different focal lengths have different uses when making images from the rim of Grand Canyon:

- Use normal lenses for photos of friends and family, for images of the canyon when there is no foreground (or the foreground is about 50 feet or more away when the needed depth of focus is not difficult to achieve), and for close-ups if the lens is equipped with a macro setting.

- Use telephoto lenses for compression of distances (making objects at varying distances appear as if they are grouped closer to one another) and for zeroing in on photogenic ridges, tree lines, and nearby buttes, converting them into larger and therefore stronger image elements. Interestingly, by using a *strong* telephoto lens you will be able to "remodel" the canyon, making it appear narrower, its terrain steeper, and its depth even more profound.

- Use wide-angle lenses to incorporate forceful foregrounds and also gain depth of focus for those foregrounds.

- Wide-angle lens caution: Don't, *just don't*, use a wide-angle lens to "squeeze" all of Grand Canyon into your photographs. Unless the frame includes extraordinarily dramatic clouds or fantastically dramatic lighting, it won't work because the canyon's colossal, majestic temples and plateaus will be reduced to specks within the image. Also, unless you are purposefully pursuing an avant-garde look, avoid the use of strong wide-angle lenses when photographing people, especially if they are located near the edge of the image frame, where their bodies (especially their heads) will be most obviously distorted.

TECHNIQUE | FOCAL LENGTH

Telephoto

Wide Angle

Wide Angle

TECHNIQUE | PATTERNS & GRAPHIC LINES

Patterns & Graphic Lines

Often the most pleasing photos are those that possess strong lines and patterns, either in the foreground or within the canyon. Make it a point to look for these structural elements.

- Watch for repeating patterns of ridges and temples in the canyon, especially at sunrise or sunset, when lighting emphasizes the simple but classic profiles of the canyon's monumental internal features.

- Railings on the rim, especially their shadows and silhouettes against a bright background, can add interesting lines and patterns.

- The Trailview Overlook on Hermit Road offers great views of the switchbacks along Bright Angel Trail. Emphasize the zigzagging patterns by moving in close with a telephoto lens.

- Tree branches and tree trunks can add interesting forms, especially if they are portrayed in silhouette against the bright sky.

- Images with powerful lines and patterns are often abstractions. In my opinion, this is one of the most expressive forms of photography because abstract images unveil inconspicuous elegance.

> One of my highest goals is to create art with my landscape photography. If I analyze what makes an image a piece of art, then I usually find it has compelling structure—it possesses a basic simplicity, a structural pattern (and sometimes a structural pattern with a flaw), parallel lines or diverging lines or concentric curves. So I look for structure in my images. You should, too.

TECHNIQUE | PATTERNS & GRAPHIC LINES

TECHNIQUE | SHADOWS & SILHOUETTES

TECHNIQUE | SHADOWS & SILHOUETTES

Shadows & Silhouettes

Sometimes it is not the object itself but the object's shadow or silhouette that is most arresting. Here are some:

- The shadows of railings at the canyon's overlooks used as foreground elements.

- People standing on the rim, both their silhouettes against the background and their shadows in the foreground.

- Tree trunks and limbs (gnarled junipers are especially appealing), their silhouettes against the bright sky or inner canyon.

- Cacti, especially prickly pear cacti with their iconic profiles.

- In the inner canyon, repeating similar-shaped shadows cast by the canyon's long ridges.

Shadows are so familiar to us that they have disappeared from our conscious perceptions. Shadows recorded in a photograph, however, especially those that are black and oddly shaped, wield far more impact because contrast in a photograph is exaggerated. Therefore, shadows appearing in photos can be used as intentional, desirable picture elements or, if they are unperceived by the photographer, they can prove to be a distraction.

> For photographic purposes, canyon attributes should be secondary. Of first priority should be color, lines, drama, foregrounds, and illumination rather than objects. Grand Canyon photos need to be treated as complete units of art.

TECHNIQUE | BACKLIGHTING

Backlighting

Looking into the sun is unnatural and potentially dangerous. But interesting photos lie sunward, most of them missed by photographers. If you know how to adjust the exposure of your camera, choose backlit scenes for drama. Being careful not to look directly at the sun, try these techniques:

- Some plants and human-related objects (especially women's scarves and hair) are translucent. When viewed from behind, the translucence can be dazzling.

TECHNIQUE | SUN STARS

Sun Stars

By using a strong wide-angle lens and a small aperture, it is possible to make a sun star, a starburst effect when the sun is included in the scene. Exposure adjustments are likely.

TECHNIQUE | GOD RAYS

God Rays

When the sun is low or below the horizon, crepuscular rays (also known as God rays) can appear in the sky or within the canyon. They radiate away from the sun even if the sun is out of view below the horizon. The effect varies from subtle to robust, but the camera's routine of capturing the world with heightened contrast can be just what is needed for a vivid rendering.

CREATING A SLIDE SHOW

Since the rise of digital photography, the definition of *slide show* has shifted. Although slides themselves are rarely seen today, the term still means showing a succession of images, only now they are shown on a computer screen or via digital projector. Here are some guidelines:

✿ Of supreme importance: Be brutal when deciding what to include. Slide shows that display too many images (good ones, fair ones, terrible ones, out-of-focus ones, mis-exposed ones, dreary ones, nearly identical ones, trite ones, etc.) are deadly. Keep it short and everyone will love your photos!

✿ Don't linger on any one image for long. This is a slide show, not a talk show.

✿ Variety is key. In most cases your viewers will want to see images of Grand Canyon in various moods, close-ups, and shots of your friends and family (standing on the rim, on hikes, and having dinner at El Tovar), buildings on the rim, animals, wide-angle shots with rim foregrounds, and telephoto shots of the inner canyon. Give 'em a taste of everything.

✿ Finally, don't include the grab shot of Dad scratching his bum.

GRAND CANYON FACTS

If you're planning to create a slide show of Grand Canyon images, it's great to include canyon facts. Here are a few:

⚙ Grand Canyon is 277 miles long, about a mile deep, and averages ten miles wide.

⚙ About 1,000 cubic miles of rock were carried away by the Colorado River to create Grand Canyon.

⚙ Because the canyon's rims are spectacularly convoluted, there are about ten times as many rim miles (2,700 miles) as river miles (277 miles).

⚙ The rock layers that appear in the walls of Grand Canyon are mostly of sedimentary origin created over a huge span of geologic time.

⚙ The oldest Grand Canyon rock, found at the bottom of the canyon, is 1.84 billion years old. The youngest rock layer, the rim rock of the canyon, is 270 million years old.

⚙ Grand Canyon was carved by the Colorado River, not by an asteroid impact, glaciers, or crustal fracturing.

⚙ The Colorado River has cut downward into the Kaibab Plateau. But the rock walls of Grand Canyon have decayed and weathered over time. Gravity, precipitation, the action of plants and animals, and the freeze-thaw cycle loosen and draw rock particles, slabs, and boulders down into the side canyons. Flash floods carry the rubble into the Colorado River, which then sweeps the debris downstream toward the Gulf of California.

⚙ Colorado River rapids most often occur at the mouths of side canyons, where flash flood debris obstructs the river. The Colorado River drops about 2,000 feet, mostly in the rapids, as it twists its way through Grand Canyon.

⚙ Most geologists believe that the canyon is about 6 million years old. (That's really young geologically, especially when compared to the canyon's rock units, which are typically hundreds of millions of years old, or more.) However, there is credible evidence that earlier canyon systems existed here before Grand Canyon. Portions of these predecessor canyons were probably incorporated into Grand Canyon, confusing the issue somewhat. But if you stipulate that the Colorado River be flowing through the Grand Canyon, then it's 6 million years old, no question.

⚙ Native Americans have explored and lived in Grand Canyon intermittently for about 12,000 years. People of European origin didn't know of Grand Canyon until one of Coronado's lieutenants, Garcia Lopez de Cardenas, was guided to the rim by Hopi Indians in 1540.

⚙ About 5 million visitors come to Grand Canyon each year.

⚙ The first documented river trip through Grand Canyon was made by John Wesley Powell and his men in 1869. Today, about 25,000 river runners make the white-water run through the canyon every year.

⚙ The first rim-bound tourists began to arrive in the 1880s. When the railroad arrived at the rim in 1901, tourism began to explode.

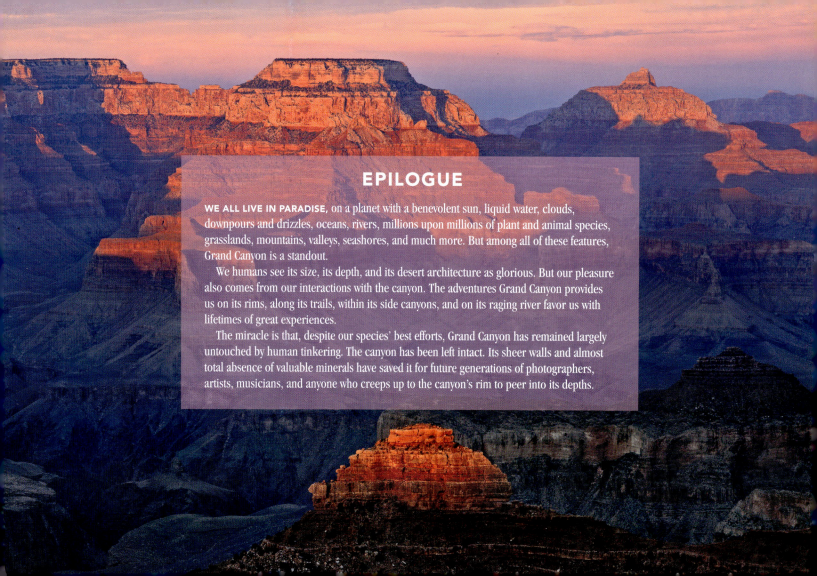

EPILOGUE

WE ALL LIVE IN PARADISE, on a planet with a benevolent sun, liquid water, clouds, downpours and drizzles, oceans, rivers, millions upon millions of plant and animal species, grasslands, mountains, valleys, seashores, and much more. But among all of these features, Grand Canyon is a standout.

We humans see its size, its depth, and its desert architecture as glorious. But our pleasure also comes from our interactions with the canyon. The adventures Grand Canyon provides us on its rims, along its trails, within its side canyons, and on its raging river favor us with lifetimes of great experiences.

The miracle is that, despite our species' best efforts, Grand Canyon has remained largely untouched by human tinkering. The canyon has been left intact. Its sheer walls and almost total absence of valuable minerals have saved it for future generations of photographers, artists, musicians, and anyone who creeps up to the canyon's rim to peer into its depths.

As the National Park Service's official charitable partner, Grand Canyon Conservancy provides private funding to enable Grand Canyon National Park to raise the margin of excellence for educational programs and preservation, build innovation in Park services, and support the necessities not currently funded by federal dollars. We invite you to join us! Visit www.grandcanyon.org.

POSTAGE REQUIRED

Point Imperial View, North Rim © 2016 by Gary Ladd

Please do not write below this line – POSTAL USE ONLY

 **GRAND CANYON CONSERVANCY**

As the National Park Service's official charitable partner, Grand Canyon Conservancy provides private funding to enable Grand Canyon National Park to raise the margin of excellence for educational programs and preservation, build innovation in Park services, and support the necessities not currently funded by federal dollars. We invite you to join us! Visit www.grandcanyon.org.

POSTAGE REQUIRED

Mather Point Rainbow, South Rim © 2016 by Gary Ladd